WHAT DOES A COW DO FOR FUN?

Goes to the mooo-vies.

WHAT DO YOU CALL A DONKEY
WITH THREE LEGS?

Wonky.

HOW DO ALL THE OCEANS SAY HELLO
TO EACH OTHER?

They wave!

WHAT'S THE DIFFERENCE BETWEEN
ELEPHANTS AND BANANAS?

Bananas are yellow.

WHAT DO YOU GET WHEN YOU POUR HOT WATER DOWN A RABBIT HOLE?

HOT CROSS BUNNIES.

WHERE DOES THE QUEEN KEEP HER ARMIES?

UP HER SLEEVIES.

WHAT DO YOU CALL A TRAIN THAT SNEEZES?

ACHOO-CHOO TRAIN.

WHY DO GIRAFFES HAVE SUCH LONG NECKS?

BECAUSE THEY HAVE SMELLY FEET.

What do you get if you cross a sheep with a kangaroo?

A Woolly Jumper.

What did the policeman say to his tummy?

You're under a vest!

Why was six scared of seven?

Because seven eight nine.

Where do you find a dog with no legs?

Where you left him.

Why are pirates called pirates?

Because they ARRRRRR.

How do you start a teddy bear race?

Ready teddy go!

Which dinosaur had to wear glasses?

Tyrannosaurus Specs!

What do you call an alligator dressed in a vest?

An investigator!

What is black and white and goes round and round?

A penguin in a tumble dryer.

WHAT'S ORANGE AND SOUNDS LIKE A
PARROT?

A CARROT.

WHO GRANTED THE FISH A WISH?

THE FAIRY CODMOTHER.

WHAT DO YOU CALL A FLY WITHOUT
WINGS?

A WALK.

WHAT DO ELVES LEARN AT SCHOOL?

THE ELF-ABET.

What do you call a fairy that doesn't like to shower?

Stinkerbell.

How do you make toast in the jungle?

Put it under a Grilla.

What is a toad's favourite drink?

Croak-a-cola.

What wobbles in the sky?

A Jelly-copter.

What's a monster's favourite game?

Swallow the leader.

WHAT DO YOU CALL A BEAR WITH NO TEETH?

A gummy bear!

WHAT DO YOU CALL A GUY LYING ON YOUR DOORSTEP?

Matt.

WHAT ANIMAL DO YOU LOOK LIKE WHEN YOU GET INTO THE BATH?

A little bear!

WHAT IS RED AND SMELLS LIKE BLUE PAINT?

Red paint.

Where do fish keep their money?

In a river bank.

What do penguins wear on their heads?

Ice caps.

What do you call a blind dinosaur?

Do-you-think-he-saurus.

Why did the banana go to the doctor?

Because it wasn't peeling well.

What do you call a sheep with no legs?

A cloud!

WHAT DO YOU CALL A GORILLA WITH BANANAS IN ITS EARS?

Anything you like, he can't hear you.

WHAT DO YOU CALL A FISH WITH NO EYES?

A fsh.

WHAT GOES "HA HA HA.....THUD!"?

A monster laughing his head off.

WHAT DO YOU CALL A BOOMERANG THAT WON'T COME BACK?

A stick.

WHAT DID ONE EYE SAY TO THE OTHER EYE?

Between us, something smells.

WHY DON'T POLAR BEARS EAT PENGUINS?

Because they can't get the wrappers off.

Do you want to hear a joke about a PIZZA?

Never mind, it's too cheesy!

How do bees brush their hair?

They use honeycombs.

What do kittens like to eat?

Mice cream.

What do you get if you cross a fish with an elephant?

Swimming trunks.

WHY DO DRAGONS SLEEP DURING THE DAY?

So they can fight knights.

WHAT'S RED AND INVISIBLE?

No tomatoes.

WHY DID THE STARFISH BLUSH?

Because the sea weed.

WHAT'S A FOOT LONG AND SLIPPERY?

A slipper.

HOW DO YOU ORGANIZE A SPACE PARTY?

Planet early.

What goes "tick, woof, tick woof"?

A watch dog.

Why do bees hum?

They've forgotten the words.

What did one tomato say to the other tomato?

You go ahead and I'll ketchup.

What is yellow and dangerous?

Shark infested custard!

How many tickles does it take to make an octopus laugh?

Ten (tickles).

WHAT TIME SHOULD YOU GO TO THE DENTIST?

TOOTH HURTY.

KNOCK, KNOCK. –WHO'S THERE?
–LITTLE OLD LADY.
–LITTLE OLD LADY WHO?
–I DIDN'T KNOW YOU COULD YODEL!

HOW DO YOU CATCH A SQUIRREL?

CLIMB A TREE AND ACT LIKE A NUT.

WHY DID THE BURGLAR TAKE A SHOWER?

HE WANTED TO MAKE A CLEAN GETAWAY.

How can you tell which rabbit is the oldest?

Look for grey hares.

Where does Tarzan buy his clothes?

At a jungle sale.

When is it bad luck to meet a black cat?

When you're a mouse.

What do you do when 50 zombies surround your house?

Hope it's Halloween!!

I started writing a story about a broken pencil, but I gave up because it was pointless.

What do you call a rich elf?

Welfy.

Two hedgehogs are in the middle of the road and they're by a zebra crossing. One says, "Don't cross here!" The other one says, "Why not?" The first one says, "Look what happened to this zebra!"

When does it rain money?

When there is "change" in the weather.

How did the yeti feel when he had flu?

Abominable.

WHAT'S THE DIFFERENCE BETWEEN MASHED POTATOES AND PEA SOUP?

Anyone can mash potatoes....

A boy asks his father, "Dad, are bugs good to eat?" "That's disgusting — don't talk about things like that over dinner," the dad replies. After dinner the father asks, "Now, son, what did you want to ask me?" "Oh, nothing," the boy says "There was a bug in your soup, but now it's gone."

HOW DOES THE MAN IN THE MOON CUT HIS HAIR?

Eclipse it.

WHY DID THE SCIENTIST WEAR DENIM?

Because he was a jean-ius.

WHAT HAPPENS WHEN COWS REFUSE TO BE MILKED?

Udder chaos.

WHAT DO YOU CALL A MAN TRAPPED IN A PAPER BAG?

Russell.

A man was taken to hospital after eating daffodil bulbs. Doctors say he's recovering and he'll be out in the Spring.

HOW ARE FALSE TEETH LIKE STARS?

They come out at night!

WHAT'S FASTER, COLD OR HOT?

HOT, BECAUSE YOU CAN CATCH A COLD.

WHO IS THE WORLD'S GREATEST
UNDERWATER SECRET AGENT?

JAMES POND.

WHY WOULDN'T THE CRAB SHARE HIS
SWEETS?

BECAUSE HE WAS A LITTLE SHELLFISH!

WHY DID THE TOILET PAPER ROLL DOWN
THE HILL?

TO GET TO THE BOTTOM.

WHAT DID THE PIG SAY ON THE BEACH?

"I'M BACON".

WHY DID THE OPERA SINGER GO ON A CRUISE?

SHE WANTED TO HIT THE HIGH Cs.

DID YOU HEAR ABOUT THE TWO GUYS WHO STOLE A CALENDAR?

THEY EACH GOT SIX MONTHS.

WHAT'S THE DIFFERENCE BETWEEN A FISH AND PIANO?

YOU CAN'T TUNA FISH.

What do you do if you see a spaceman?

Park your car, man.

What do you call a man with a large flat fish on his head?

Ray!

What does the King do when he burps?

He issues a royal pardon.

Why didn't the skeleton go to the party?

Because he had no body to go with.

Where do sheep go on holiday?

To the Baaaaa-hamas.

WHAT IS IT CALLED WHEN A CAT WINS A
DOG SHOW?

A CAT-HAS-TROPHY.

WHAT DO YOU CALL AN EXPLODING MONKEY?

A BAB-BOOM.

WHAT HAPPENED WHEN THE OWL LOST HER
VOICE?

SHE DIDN'T GIVE A HOOT.

WHY ARE GHOSTS SO BAD AT LYING?

BECAUSE YOU CAN SEE RIGHT THROUGH THEM!

HOW DO YOU HELP AN INJURED PIG?

CALL A HAMBULANCE.

What do you call a French man in sandals?

Phillipe Phloppe.

I wrote a song about a tortilla. Well actually, it's more of a rap.

What do you call a girl who stands inside goalposts and stops the ball rolling away?

Annette.

My friend thinks he is smart. He told me an onion is the only food that makes you cry, so I threw a coconut at him.

WHAT DO YOU CALL A FAKE NOODLE?

AN IMPASTA.

WAITER! WAITER! THIS COFFEE TASTES
LIKE SOIL.

YES, SIR, IT WAS GROUND THIS MORNING.

WHAT DO YOU CALL A STAG WITH NO
EYES?

NO EYE-DEER.

WHAT DO YOU CALL A STAG WITH NO EYES
AND NO LEGS?

STILL NO EYE-DEER.

WHAT VEGETABLES DO LIBRARIANS LIKE?

QUIET PEAS.

WHY DID THE SCARECROW GET A PAY RISE?

Because he was outstanding in his field.

WHERE DO ALIENS GO TO GET DRUNK?

To a Mars Bar.

WHY DID THE SCIENTIST INSTALL A KNOCKER ON HIS DOOR?

He wanted to win the No-bell prize.

WHAT DO NINJAS EAT FOR LUNCH?

Kung-food.

WHAT DO YOU CALL A SNAKE ON A BUILDING SITE?

A boa constructor.

What is the smartest insect?

A Spelling Bee.

What lies at the bottom of the ocean, worrying?

A nervous wreck.

Why do seagulls fly over the sea?

Because if they flew over the bay, they would be baygulls!

What did one plate say to the other?

Dinner is on me!

My friend recently got crushed by a pile of books but he's only got his shelf to blame.

What do you call a dinosaur with a extensive vocabulary?

A thesaurus.

Why did Luke Skywalker always sleep with the light on?

He was afraid of the Darth.

Two silk worms had a race. It ended in a tie.

What did the llama say when he got kicked out of the zoo?

"Alpaca my bags!"

How do stop an astronaut's baby crying?

You rocket!

How do you make gold soup?
Put in 14 carrots.

If you're English in the kitchen and English in the living room, what are you in the bathroom?
European.

If a butcher wears a size XL shirt and a size 13 shoe, what does he weigh?
Meat.

What gives you the power to walk through a wall?
A door.

How do you make gold soup?
Put in 14 carrots.

If you're English in the kitchen and English in the living room, what are you in the bathroom?
European.

If a butcher wears a size XL shirt and a size 13 shoe, what does he weigh?
Meat.

What gives you the power to walk through a wall?
A door.

How to bears keep cool?

They use bear-conditioning.

What happens when you wear a snow suit inside?

It melts all over the carpet.

Why are fish so intelligent?

Because they're always in schools.

Why did the man put his money in the freezer?

He wanted cold hard cash.

What kind of tree fits in your hand?

A palm tree!

If you are an astronaut and you don't end every relationship with "I just need space" then you are wasting everyone's time.

Vincent van Gough walks into a bar, and the bartender offers him a drink... No thank you, said Vincent, I've got one 'ere.

A policeman caught a nasty little boy with a BB gun in one hand and a lizard in the other. "Now Listen here," the policeman said, "Whatever you do to that poor, defenceless creature I shall personally do to you" "In that case," said the boy, "I'll kiss its butt and let it go"

A kid threw a lump of cheddar at me. I thought "That's not very mature".

What does a nosy pepper do?

Gets jalapeno business.

I hate Russian dolls. They're so full of themselves.

Why do ducks make good detectives?

They always quack the case!

Never trust an atom. They make up everything.

Why do French people like to eat snails?

They can't stand fast food.

A recent scientific study showed that out of 2,293,618,367 people, 94% are too lazy to actually read that number.

What did the envelope say to the stamp?
Stick with me and we'll go places!

Two clairvoyants meet. One says to the other: "You are fine, and how am I?

Why can't your nose be twelve inches long?
Because then it would be a foot.

I hated my job as an origami teacher. Too much paperwork.

I love pressing F5. It's so refreshing.

Why did the computer go to the doctor?

Because it had a virus.

A dog walks into a job centre. 'Wow, a talking dog,' says the clerk. 'With your talent I'm sure we can find you a gig in the circus.' 'The circus?' says the dog. 'What does a circus want with a plumber?'

My girlfriend has just dumped me because she thinks I'm obsessed with football. I'm gutted — we'd been going out for three seasons.

What breed of dog do magicians own?

Labra-cadabra-dors!

I went to a restaurant with a sign that said they served breakfast at any time. So I ordered scrambled eggs during the Renaissance.

The other day my friend was telling me that I didn't understand irony.....Which is ironic because we were standing at a bus stop.

What's the best part about living in Switzerland?

Not sure, but the flag is a big plus.

Someone stole my mood ring. I'm not sure how I feel about that.

What do you get when you cross a joke with a rhetorical question?

My new hobby is eating clocks. It's rather time-consuming.

Did you hear about the hyena that swallowed an Oxo cube?

He made a laughing stock of himself.

I bought the world's worst thesaurus yesterday. Not only is it terrible, it's terrible.

Have you heard about corduroy pillows? They're making headlines.

Sometimes I tuck my knees into my chest and lean forward. That's just how I roll.

What do you call a cow without a map?
Udderly lost!

Why did the robot go on a summer holiday?
He needed to recharge his batteries.

Why can't you hear a pterodactyl in the bathroom?
Because it has a silent pee.

The past, present and future walked into a bar. It was tense.

A lot of people cry when they cut an onion. The trick is not to form an emotional bond.

I hate people who use big words just to make themselves look perspicacious.

How do you drown a Hipster?
In the mainstream.

People are always telling me to live my dreams.
But I don't want to be naked in an exam I haven't revised for.

Why do rappers need umbrellas?
Fo' drizzle.

What's the difference between ignorance and apathy?

I don't know, and I don't care.

What did one DNA strand say to the other?

Does my bum look big in these genes?

What did the grape say when he was pinched?

Nothing, he gave a little wine.

I thought my neighbours were lovely people. Then they went and put a password on their wi-fi.

What's the difference between ignorance and apathy?

I don't know, and I don't care.

What did one DNA strand say to the other?

Does my bum look big in these genes?

What did the grape say when he was pinched?

Nothing, he gave a little wine.

I thought my neighbours were lovely people. Then they went and put a password on their wi-fi.

A police recruit was asked during the exam, "What would you do if you had to arrest your own mother?" He said, "Call for backup."

I've just opened a new restaurant called Karma. There's no menu, we just give you what you deserve.

I thought I'd tell you a brilliant time-travel joke, but you didn't like it.

My boss told me yesterday, "You shouldn't dress for the job you have, dress for the job you want". But when I turned up today in Ghostbusters clothes, he said I was fired.

Where do you learn to make ice cream?

At sundae school!

What kind of magazines do cows read?

Cattlelogs!

Why did the scarecrow win an award?

Because he was outstanding in his field!

How do you fix a pumpkin with a hole in it?

With a pumpkin patch!

How do you spell "candy" with just two letters?

C and Y.

What do you call a man with a rubber toe?

Roberto.

What does a house wear?

Address!

When is a car not a car?

When it turns into a driveway!

What happens when frogs park illegally?

They get toad.

Why are pediatricians always so angry?

Because they have little patients.

How can you tell an alligator from a crocodile?

By paying attention to whether the animal will see you later, or after a while.

What days are the strongest?

Saturday and Sunday. The rest are week (weak) days!

What's the leading cause of dry skin?

Towels.

Why do cows have bells?

Because their horns don't work.

What do you call a cow with no legs?

Ground beef!

What sort of room has no windows or doors?

A mushroom!

Why don't crabs give to charity?

Because they are shellfish!

Why do melons have weddings?

Because they cantaloupe.

What do you call a dinosaur with an extensive vocabulary?

A thesaurus.

What do lazy farmers grow?

Couch potatoes!

WHY DOES A CHICKEN COOP ONLY HAVE TWO DOORS?

BECAUSE IF IT HAD FOUR DOORS IT WOULD BE A CHICKEN SEDAN!

WHAT'S THE DIFFERENCE BETWEEN AN AFRICAN ELEPHANT AND AN INDIAN ELEPHANT?

ABOUT 5,000 MILES.

WHAT DO YOU CALL A PIG THAT DOES KARATE?

A PORK CHOP!

HOW MANY APPLES GROW ON A TREE?

ALL OF THEM.

Printed in Great Britain
by Amazon

24103141R00051